IT'S A
GIRL!

MARIANNE RICHMOND

Published by Sourcebooks, Inc.
P.O. Box 4410, Naperville, Illinois 60567-4410
(630) 961-3900
Fax: (630) 961-2168
www.sourcebooks.com

Printed and bound in China.

LEO 10 9 8 7 6 5 4 3 2 1

To: _Olivia Grace_

From: _Aunt Shannon_
Uncle Richard &
Family

It's a

Girl!

What a wonderful blessing.

Her ten
tiny fingers.

Sweet, kissable toes.

Chubby, cherubic cheeks
and cute button nose.

Did you ever think

someone so *little*

could make you feel love…

so BIG?

Delight in the "girly-ness" of it all.

Cuddly pink sleepers.
Cute jeans and dresses.

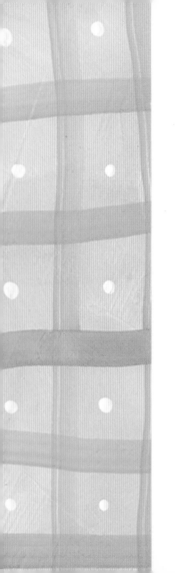

Tiny, shiny shoes.

Bows in her tresses.

There is nothing
so innocent,

∽

so heartwarming, as
little girl playtime.

Dress up.
Midday parties with doll friends.
Silly dancing.

And loving anything sparkly!

She'll endear you with her "me-do-it" resolve,

wide-ranging emotions,
cuddles to spare,

and everyday notions.

Teach her early that it's "ladies' choice" out there.

Encourage her to go for it, whether it be soccer or softball or dance. Reading…or math.

Girls hurt easily.

Handle her with care.

Make time for her.

Listen to her.

Celebrate her.

Pray for her.

Tell her how very beautiful she is…

inside and outside.

And how the inside
matters more.

Tell her how much she's loved—whatever her mood.

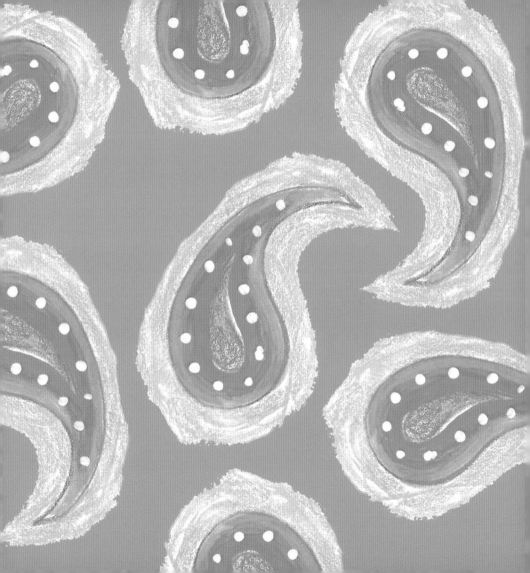

Teach her self-respect

and boundaries.

Kindness, manners,
and self-sufficiency.

Make time for the important stuff.

Piggyback rides. Hopscotch.

Mud pies. Freeze tag. Jump rope.

Making a wish. Underdogs.

Help her grow into a young woman
who loves herself just the way she is!

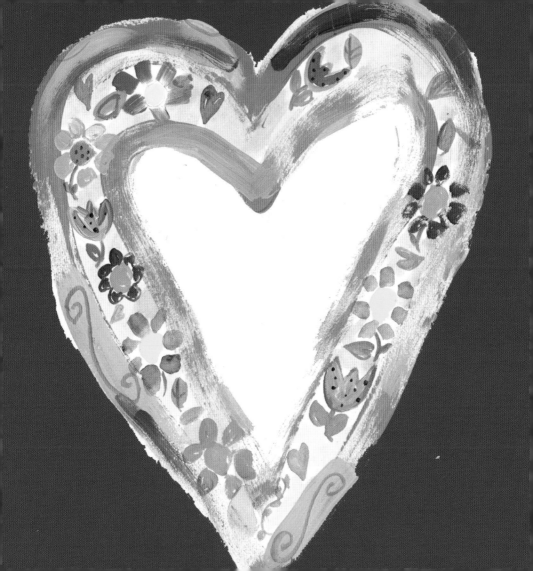

Cherish the journey and
the adventure of parenthood.

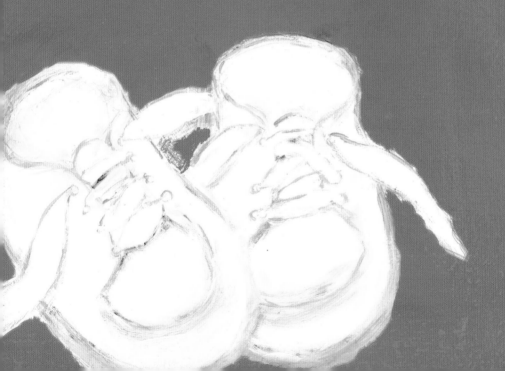

The gifts will be many,
the lessons innumerable,
the love all consuming.

It's a

Girl!

What an *incredible* blessing.

About the Author

Beloved author and artist Marianne Richmond has touched the lives of millions for nearly two decades through her award-winning books, greeting cards, and other gift products that offer people the most heartfelt way to connect with each other. She lives in the Minneapolis area. Visit www.mariannerichmond.com.